BUYIN' TROUBLE

REAL ESTATE RESCUE COZY MYSTERIES, BOOK
13

PATTI BENNING

SUMMER PRESCOTT BOOKS PUBLISHING

CHAPTER ONE

Flora stared at the keys on the table in front of her, hardly able to believe the long, frustrating process of buying a house was over.

This was it. She was officially a homeowner. Again.

"Congratulations, Ms. Abner," the closing agent said. "Enjoy your new home. Do you have any further questions?"

It was a busy day at the title company, judging from the people who had been waiting in the foyer when she and the man she had bought the house from, Mason Mitchell, arrived. She had the feeling the closing agent was trying to politely encourage her to leave, so she decided to put off her little mental celebration until later. She snatched up the keys and the folder of paperwork she would have to take home and store somewhere safe, and rose to her feet. Across the table, Mr. Mitchell did the same, and followed her out of the room.

The past few weeks had been a whirlwind of activity, between her aunt purchasing and gifting the first house Flora had planned on flipping back to her, and a myriad of meetings with banks and real estate agents as she transferred the money she owed her aunt for the loan she had received two years ago, and started the process of buying her second house to flip.

But now, finally, all of that was done, and she could focus on the brand-new project in front of her.

And what a project it was.

The cozy farmhouse that was now her forever home had been a breeze to fix up in comparison to the little yellow house she had just purchased. She was glad she had started easy, but she hoped she hadn't bitten off more than she could chew this time around.

"Ms. Abner?"

She turned around on the sidewalk just outside of the title company. Mr. Mitchell was standing behind her. He was an older man, in his sixties or early seventies with a shiny bald patch on top of his head and kind blue eyes, and he had sold her the house for a rock bottom price, so she was more than happy to chat with him for a few minutes if that was what he wanted.

"You can go ahead and call me Flora," she said. "Thank you again for everything."

"I'm just glad the house is going to end up in good hands." He sighed, his gaze going distant. "I never should have let things get as bad as they did. If there's one piece of advice I could give to the younger generations, it would be to treasure your memory while you have it. I can't tell you how many times I thought I scheduled a repair only to realize too late that I'd let it go too long. You'll take care of the place, won't you?"

"I'll get it looking better than ever before you know it," she promised.

"That's what I want to hear." He nodded at her, then glanced behind her. "I think that's Jonah, my son, so I'd better go. Don't want to keep him waiting. You have a nice day now, Flora."

She heard the sound of a car pulling up along the curb before he finished speaking, and turned around to see a dusty tan sedan with its windows rolled down. A man about her own age with long, dark blond hair pulled back into a pony tail was leaning across the front seat, looking at her through the passenger window.

"Are you the lady that bought the house?" he called out. She nodded, and he gave her a big thumbs up. "Good luck with it! I grew up there, before my dad let it get all run down. Maybe when you finish repairing it, I could pop by for a tour?"

"Sure," she said. "It might be a while, but I'll try to remember to look you up."

He grinned, then shoved the passenger door open for his father and stopped leaning so far over. Flora watched as the two of them pulled away. She hoped she could do the house justice for them. It was going to be a lot of work, but in a year or two, it would make a lovely home for someone. The town of Warbler, Kentucky would have one less run-down wreck of a house. She might not be changing the world, but breathing new life into houses felt like a worthy goal.

The new house was inside the town limits of Warbler, unlike the farmhouse. Nestled on a residential street near the outskirts of town, it was smack dab in the middle of the block, with houses on all sides. It had yellow siding, which would be cheery once she cleaned it up a little, and a fenced in back yard. Both the front and the back yards were horribly overgrown, and there were even plants growing in the gutters.

The short blacktop driveway was cracked and

filled with weeds, and the door to the detached garage hung crookedly, stuck shut. Two of the windows on the first floor were broken and boarded over.

The house was an eyesore. It looked like it had been abandoned for years, which wasn't far from the truth. It had also been cheaper than a new car to buy, and Flora could already envision how it would look when she was done with it.

Still, as she sat there in the driveway, looking up at the house she now owned, she felt a tingle of doubt. Had she gotten in over her head?

No. She might be part-owner of the local hardware store, but that was just a side job. Flipping houses was her *career*, or what she wanted her career to be, at least. She might have to spend every waking hour working her fingers to the bone to get this house how she envisioned it, but by golly, she was going to do it.

A light knock on her truck's window made her jolt. She had been so lost in her contemplation of the house that she hadn't even noticed the man approaching. He had shaggy grey hair and a stained t-shirt, but his smile was friendly, and Flora rolled the window down.

"How can I help you?" she asked politely.

"Are you the new owner?" he asked, nodding at the house.

"I am. How did you know?"

He pointed at the sign in the yard, which had changed from *For Sale* to *Pending*, and would probably change to *Sold* by this time tomorrow, or whenever the agent got a chance to stop by. "Don't know why anyone else would be gazing at this garbage heap. My name's Wyatt Cooper, I'm your neighbor."

He waved at a house with wooden shake siding across the street with an odd assortment of garden gnomes in the yard, then held out a hand, which she shook.

"I'm Flora," she said. "It's nice to meet you."

"You're a brave lady, buying this place," he said. "You've seen the inside, right? It's a wreck."

"I know, but I'm prepared for it."

"If you say so. Me and my wife, Willow, we're both retired, so if you need anything, you can come on over and ask us. Are you planning on moving in right away?"

"I'm actually not planning on moving in at all," she explained. She wished she had been able to get out of the truck before talking to him, because it was awkward to sit here and look up at him while they chatted, but he was standing too close to the door for her to open it without asking him to move. "I'm going to flip the house. I'll fix it up and then sell it to someone who wants to live in it."

"Sounds like a lot of hard work," he said. "I'll keep an eye on the place for you, though. I've been doing it for Mason long enough, I'm used to it. I've chased away more than a few troublemakers. Folk see an empty house and think no one cares if they mess around inside it."

"Thanks," Flora said. Once again, she wondered if she was in over her head. She was prepared for the repairs, but she hadn't even thought about having to deal with people breaking into the house. "Can I give you my number, so you can call me if there's any trouble?"

He took his cell phone out of his pocket and they exchanged numbers. He left her with a final, cheery "Good luck!" and finally, she opened her truck's door and slipped out. It was time to get to know her new house.

CHAPTER TWO

The house had a few positive aspects. The roof, for one. It was only a few years old, and according to the house inspector, would be good for decades to come.

The locks were another. They had been changed recently – Wyatt's mention of break-ins might explain that, now that she thought about it – and the door opened without a complaint. She stepped through, onto bare sub-flooring.

The bones of the house were the third good thing about it. The structure was strong, the foundation was whole and uncracked, and the floors were solid.

But that was where the good traits ended. The house's interior had been gutted. The floors were bare plywood, and the walls and ceilings had been stripped of their drywall, leaving behind bare insulation and wiring. The house didn't even have a furnace, or a water heater. The only thing that worked in it was the electricity.

She looked around the room she had stepped into. It had probably once been a living room; even if it hadn't been, it was going to *become* a living room by the time she was done with it. It was a spacious room, taking up the entire width of the front of the house, with four windows – two of which looked out over the front yard, and the other two looked into the side yard on either side of the house. The two leftmost windows were boarded over.

Flora shut the door behind her and walked down the hall. A door on the right led to a bathroom. The plumbing was there, but no fixtures. It was a full bath, with room for a bathtub against the wall, with a window on it.

Opposite the bathroom was a linen closet, and further down the hall were two more doorways. One led to what must have been a laundry room, and the other led to the kitchen.

The kitchen was the only room in the house that hadn't been completely stripped of everything, but the half-torn down cupboards and broken pieces of the counter were worse than an empty room would have been. There was a sliding glass door that led from a dining nook to a small, rickety looking back porch. In the corner opposite the sliding door were the stairs.

Flora had already looked through the house, of course, but it felt different knowing that it was *hers* now, so she took her time with it, inspecting the kitchen and looking into the overgrown back yard before making her way up the bare stairs. There was no railing, so she kept one hand ready to grab at the wall studs if she slipped.

Upstairs were two bedrooms and a half bath. The larger of the two bedrooms was at the back of the house, with a nice view of the yard and the big oak tree that gave the house shade, and a window that looked out over the side yard, with an old trellis beneath it. The other bedroom was only slightly smaller and looked out onto the front yard and the street. The small upstairs bathroom had a window as well, this one looking into the side yard. One of the things she liked about the house was how many windows it had. Paired with the yellow siding, she thought the house would be bright and cheerful when she was done with it... though that was a long way off.

The house had a lot of closets, too. She wandered back into the largest bedroom and opened the door that led to a walk-in closet. The switch on the wall showed her a space a little larger than the bathroom at the farmhouse. Each room had at least one closet, from the coat closet in the living room to the cupboard in what would become the laundry room. She had a suspicion the closets would be a big draw – after all, who didn't like having plenty of closet space?

Her eyes caught on something in the back of the big closet. On the ceiling were two two-by-fours nailed over what looked like a trap door. An attic? The inspector hadn't been able to locate the attic, and said it was possible it had been sealed off after the roof was replaced. She hadn't given it much thought, but she had to admit she was a little curious.

She examined the boards, then went back downstairs to her truck to grab a hammer to pull the nails out. She grabbed a step ladder too, and carried the tools back up the stairs, feeling a thrill at the thought that she was officially starting work on the house. Sure, she was doing this mostly out of curiosity, but it had to be done. She couldn't flip the house without checking the attic; if there was some sort of issue with the roof or the insulation, she had to know.

She set up the step ladder and climbed up it, the hammer in one hand. The angle was awkward, but she managed to pry the nails out of the boards after some effort. She let the boards drop to the floor, but tucked the nails into her pocket and then set the hammer down on the top step of the ladder and pushed the trap door up.

The square section of wood moved, but not enough. After examining it for a moment, she realized it probably opened out. There was a small hole on one side, as if some sort of handle had once been nailed or screwed there, but it was long since gone.

She had a hammer, though, and if there was one thing she had learned these past few years, it was her way around a hammer. She wedged the clawed end in the gap between the trap door and the rest of the ceiling boards and slowly pulled it down.

She was right; it *was* an attic door. The hinges squealed as she slowly opened it with the hammer, but it went easier as soon as she had enough room to wedge her fingers into the gap and could really put her weight behind it. Bits of insulation fell down onto her face and hair, and she screwed her eyes shut but kept at it.

There was an awkward moment where she had to move the step ladder aside without letting go of the trap door, since it kept threatening to spring back up, but finally she got it all the way down and could see a folded wooden ladder attached to it. She unfolded it, and the weight of the ladder overpowered the springs so the door finally stopped trying to shut on its own.

Then she had easy access to the attic, just waiting for her to ascend. She gazed up into the dark square over her head, feeling suddenly unsure.

It was just an attic. There was no way it was anywhere close to being as creepy as the basement at home, and she barely even felt uncomfortable doing the laundry down there anymore, flickering lights and all.

And the attic had been boarded up, anyway. It wasn't like anyone could actually be up there. It would just be here, a bunch of insulation, some spiders, and if she was really unlucky, a few mice.

"No way am I calling Grady because I'm too afraid to go into a dark attic alone," she muttered to herself.

Slipping her phone out of her back pocket, she turned the flashlight on and started climbing the wooden ladder. The contraption sagged and squealed alarmingly, but it held, and soon her head crested the entrance. She raised her hand and shone the light around.

It was almost disappointing to see what looked like a normal attic space. It spanned the length and width of the house, the peaked ceiling just tall enough for her to stand in the center, with pink rolls of insulation between each wooden support. Her phone's light revealed a couple old moving boxes against one wall, but the rest of the space was empty... other than for the dust, and what she seriously hoped were old raisins and not rat poop.

It wasn't creepy at all. In fact, it was pretty nice, as far as attics went. As she climbed the rest of the way up, she wondered why it had been boarded over. For all she knew, this had been Mason's son's room, and he had been afraid of the attic as a kid. Maybe they had boarded it over for him, or because the door was drafty, or any number of reasons.

Finally on her feet in the center of the attic, she looked around for a light bulb, but didn't see one. Maybe she would install a simple light fixture up here; it was more storage space, and the house didn't have a basement, so a place to store boxes and bed frames would probably be welcome.

Since she was up there already, she decided to check out the boxes and see what was in them. Brushing aside a few cobwebs, she made her way to the far side of the attic and crouched near one of the smaller boxes. It was heavy when she pulled it toward her, and she was unsurprised to find it full of old books when she opened the top. Old comic books.

Maybe they were worth something; it sure would be nice if she found an old collectible worth millions up here, though she doubted she would be *that* lucky.

Pushing the box aside to look through later, she rose up on her knees and tugged at the flaps of the larger box. Something had chewed a hole through one of them, and she had a feeling whatever was in the box was destroyed by whatever rodents had made it home. This box was a three foot by three-foot cube, and the top was taped shut, instead of just folded in on itself. Grumbling, she tore the old cardboard and finally opened the top.

She was disappointed to see nothing but a grimy black garbage bag when she shone her light inside. It was covering something lumpy that she suspected were old linens, but she still wanted to see.

Holding the phone in her left hand to give her light, she pulled the garbage bag away. It wasn't wrapped around whatever was in the box; it was just sitting on top. The interior of the box was lined with some sort of plastic sheeting, she saw now, and it crinkled as she moved the garbage bag to the side.

A skull stared up at her.

Flora screamed and jolted backward, dropping her flashlight and plunging herself into sudden darkness – the phone must have landed light-side down. Something in the box rustled and she let out a weak moan of fear as she felt around for her phone. Finally, her hand knocked into it, and as soon as she turned it over, light flooded the attic once more.

She sent a terrified glance toward the box just in time to see something fist-sized with a long, naked tail leap over the edge and bound away to where the eaves touched the floor.

A rat. Her pounding heart calmed just a hair as she stared after it, then she slowly rose to her knees and aimed her light into the box again, already prepared to laugh off being so startled by what was probably just an old Halloween decoration.

But what stared back at her was undeniably real. A skeleton, with long dark hair still attacked to its head, and the tattered, chewed on remains of a dress over its bony torso. She could see a floral pattern between the dark stains on it.

A skeleton, tucked into plastic sheeting, folded into a box, and hidden away in a boarded off attic.

Flora started to silently back away toward the attic door. A torn apart kitchen and no furnace she could handle, but a skeleton in a box was a lot more than she had signed up for.

CHAPTER THREE

Flora huddled in her truck, checking yet again that the doors were locked before craning her head to look down the street. She had made it out of the house in record time and wasn't planning on leaving the safety of her truck until the police showed up.

Sure, the body looked like it had been there for a while, but she wasn't taking any chances. *She* wasn't going to end up stuffed into a box in her own attic next to that skeleton if she had anything to say about it.

A skeleton. For a second, she was right back in front of the box, on her knees, staring at the ghastly thing hidden inside. She shivered, goosebumps covering her arms despite the fact that it was early summer and the sun was beating down on the truck.

Maybe buying this house hadn't been such a good deal after all.

After what seemed like hours but had probably only been fifteen minutes at most, she saw flashing lights out of the corner of her eye and turned her head to see a police cruiser approaching. There was no siren. It wasn't an emergency – the body in her attic was long past any hope of saving. She took a deep breath, wished she had brought a bottle of water with her when she left her house this morning, and got out of her truck just as the police cruiser pulled into the driveway behind it. She was glad to see Officer Hendricks in the driver's seat, though she didn't know the name of the younger officer beside him in the passenger seat. She walked forward to meet them as they got out of the car.

"Are you all right, Ms. Abner?" Officer Hendricks asked. His concerned look made her wonder exactly how bad she looked. Her face must be reflecting her shock and horror. "Nothing else happened in the time it took us to get here?"

"I'm fine," she said. "I've just been waiting in my truck."

"Then I'm going to ask you to keep doing that while Stephen and I check the premises," he told her, all business but not unkind. "After the preliminary investigation, I'll come back out and ask you some questions. Will you be comfortable waiting out here, or would you like an escort to the station?"

"I'll be all right," she said. "I'm just a little thirsty." She swallowed. Her mouth felt very dry. It was mostly the aftereffects of the adrenaline that had coursed through her body when she realized what the box was holding, but the hot day didn't help.

"We have some water bottles in the car," he said. "I'll get you set up with one, then you just sit tight. All right?"

She nodded. In no time at all, she found herself back in her truck, a lukewarm bottle of water in her hand, and the windows rolled down halfway. She was content to wait, no matter how long it took. More than content – she was grateful for the time to collect herself. She sipped her water, leaned her seat back a little, and tried to think about what she was going to do next. Work on the house would have to wait, of course. What if there were more bodies hidden somewhere? A part of her wanted to dismiss that idea as ridiculous, but the thought of a body being hidden in the attic in the first place was just as unbelievable. Unbelievable things seemed to happen to her far too often for comfort.

This time, she kept an eye on the time, and it was

nearly half an hour later that Officer Hendricks came back out of the house. He gestured to her, and she got out of the truck, shutting the door quietly behind her. She glanced over her shoulder at Wyatt's house and wondered if he and his wife were watching through one of their windows. Some first impression she was making on her new neighbors.

"Before we start on the reason I'm here, can you confirm that you own this house? The dispatcher added that in her notes, but if I remember correctly, the last time we spoke, you told me you were keeping your farmhouse."

"I own them both now," she explained. "I'm going to sell this one as soon as I fix it up. I'm trying to make a career out of flipping houses."

She couldn't actually remember if she had ever told him about her plans. He took it in stride and pulled a little notebook out of his pocket to scribble on, giving a brief nod when he was done. "Now for the hard part. Please walk me through what happened earlier today."

Taking a deep breath, she did so, starting by telling him about spotting the boarded-up attic. He interrupted her to ask where she put the boards, which she told him, and she also handed over the four nails she had in her pocket, which he put in a little plastic baggie. Then she told him about exploring the attic, opening the small box first and then the big one, and the huge rat that had scurried out of it. She had to reach back into her truck for the water bottle and take a sip of water, her mouth suddenly dry again as she fought back a shiver.

"Did you see anything in the house that seemed out of place?" he asked when she was done. "Any evidence of a break-in or theft?"

She shook her head. "Other than the two broken windows, not really, and I think those have been broken for a while." She paused. "The guy who lives across the street mentioned that there have been issues with break-ins in the past."

She gave him Wyatt's name and pointed out the house he'd told her was his. Officer Hendricks noted the information down and told her he would speak with him when he was done talking to her. She felt a little bad about interrupting his day with an unexpected conversation with the police, but hopefully he wouldn't hold it against her.

Before he could ask her his next question, the door to the house opened and the younger officer, who Officer Hendricks had called Stephen, came out. He had something in an evidence bag in his hand and a serious expression on his face. Officer Hendricks stepped away from her, turning his back to confer with Stephen, though they weren't far enough away for any real privacy. She wasn't *trying* to eavesdrop, but she could hear them both clearly.

"There was a purse under the body," the younger officer murmured. "With an ID still in it."

"Did you get a name?" Officer Hendricks asked quietly.

Flora fought the urge to inch closer to hear them better. When Stephen responded, his voice was so quiet she almost didn't catch it. "Annabelle Morgan. I recognized the name from our cold case files."

"She's been missing for a decade," Officer. Hendricks murmured. "We'll have to wait for forensics to make a positive ID, but I've got a feeling it's not going to be a cold case for much longer. Make sure you document *everything*. It's going to be hard to pin down a suspect after so long, but I'm darn well going to try."

The younger officer nodded and hurried back into the house, and Officer Hendricks turned back to her. He eyed her for a moment, probably realizing she had overheard most of that.

"You're full of surprises, Ms. Abner. I'm sure by now you are aware that you won't be able to access this house until our forensics team is through with it.

Is there anything you need to remove from the premises before you leave?"

The only items she had in there were her stepladder and her hammer, but she didn't particularly feel like going back in to get them.

"No," she said. "Just let me know when I can come back. Do you need anything else from me right now?"

He shook his head. "Just try to stay out of trouble. This was a major case a while back, and the town is going to go crazy when we release the news about the body. We'll do our best to keep your name out of it, but there are never any guarantees. Take care of yourself." He hesitated, glanced back at the cheerful yellow house, then said, "I know this might not be the time for it, but congrats on the purchase of your house."

She wrinkled her nose but thanked him anyway, and he moved the squad car for her so she could back out of the driveway. She waved a brief goodbye to him, then pulled away down the quiet road. Not toward home, but toward the hardware store. She didn't want to be alone right now. She wasn't sure she would ever want to be alone again. The attic was going to feature in her nightmares for a long time to come.

CHAPTER FOUR

The hardware store was a home away from home for Flora. It was one of the very first places she had gone when she moved to Warbler, and ever since that first day, it had been a big part of her life.

Now she was part-owner of the store and couldn't imagine life without it. Helping Grady purchase the business was a leap of faith she was glad she had taken. She had just started dating him when they bought the store together, and there were so many ways things could have gone wrong, but for once, everything had gone right.

When she arrived, Grady was behind the counter, but to her surprise, he wasn't the only one. His brother, Wade, was there as well, and the two of them were looking over some sort of spreadsheet together. They both looked up when the bell over the door rang, and Wade gave her a cheerful wave when he recognized her. Grady mirrored the motion at first, but then his eyebrows pulled together and his hand fell back to his side as he took in her expression.

"What's wrong? Did the sale fall through?"

Of course. The sale. Somehow, even though it had barely been two hours, it felt like she had received the keys to her new house a very long time ago.

"No," she said, leaning against the other side of the counter. "That went fine. But when I got to the house…" She hesitated, glancing at Wade. But there was no reason to keep it from him, not really. He was Grady's brother, and she had been getting to know him better as time went on. Sure, he had been in prison, but the evidence that had sent him there was planted. He was trustworthy… right? "Do we have any customers?"

"Not right now," Grady said. "What happened?"

"I found a body…"

She gave them a hurried account of her discovery of the skeleton. They both looked horrified, but while Wade's expression was laced with surprise, Grady just looked resigned.

"I should've been there with you," he muttered.

"I'm sorry you had to go through that alone. Are you going to be all right?"

She hugged her arms to herself, cupping her elbows, and forced herself not to shudder even as she said, "Yeah, I'll be all right. More all right than *she* is, anyway. I can't stop thinking about it – that poor woman. Her body was hidden up there for a decade. It's so horrible."

"I thought you said it was a skeleton," Wade said. "How could you tell it was a woman?"

Grady elbowed him, but Flora didn't mind answering. Talking these things through seemed to help her. "Well, she was wearing a dress and she had long hair, but what really cinched it was when one of the officers found a purse hidden under her body with an ID in it. They still need to formally identify the body, I guess, but it sounds like her name was Annabelle Morgan, and she went missing ten years ago."

Grady frowned in sympathy, but to Flora's surprise, Wade took a step back and his eyes widened with pure shock. "Annabelle Morgan? Are you sure?"

"Well, that was the name on the ID, according to one of the officers. Like I said, they still haven't formally—"

"*You* found Annabelle Morgan?"

He stared at her in such shock that she glanced to Grady, but Grady seemed just as confused as she was. "The name's a little familiar," he admitted, turning to his brother. "Did you know her or something?"

"You don't remember? Annabelle Morgan, man. She was my boss's daughter. Remember when I worked at that warehouse? A few months before I got laid off, Mr. Morgan's daughter went missing. She was in her twenties and had just gotten back from college. Her disappearance was a big deal all over town. I wasn't the best man in the world back then, but I wasn't a complete monster either, and I remember seeing her picture posted up everywhere and hoping she was found safe and well. Felt bad for my boss. He was a jerk, but he didn't deserve losing his kid, you know?"

Grady frowned more. "It's coming back to me, but I guess I wasn't as involved as you were. They never found out what happened to her?"

"I met her a few times," Wade said. He ran a hand over his close-cut, thinning hair, still looking uncomfortable. "She came into the warehouse sometimes to visit her father, and I remember she was dating this guy…" He snapped his fingers, trying to think of the name. "James? Jones… Jonah, I think? Anyway, Mr. Morgan thought he might've had something to do with it when she vanished, but the police never arrested anyone."

"Jonah Mitchell?" Flora asked. It all seemed to line up. Jonah looked like he was in his thirties now, which meant he would have been in his twenties a decade ago. When both brothers looked at her in surprise, she added, "I bought the house from Mason Mitchell, and his son, Jonah, came to pick him up from the title company. He mentioned he grew up in the house that I bought. Considering that's where I found her body... Well, maybe he *did* have something to do with her disappearance after all."

To her surprise, Wade frowned. "I don't know about that. Now, I didn't know him that well, but he always seemed a bit too normal to have done something like that. Not exactly the type of person to murder a lady and shove her body into a box for a decade."

"Killers don't go around with their crimes tattooed on their foreheads," Grady muttered. "What do you expect a murderer to look like?"

"You show me one cold-blooded killer who went around wearing khaki pants and polo shirts, I'll wait," Wade said, crossing his arms.

Grady mirrored the position. "Haven't you ever

watched a crime show? That description fits a lot of killers."

"Look, killing someone and hiding their body and keeping quiet about it for a decade is only something a psycho would do," Wade argued. "And I can always tell when someone isn't quite right in the head. Jonah was as normal as they came."

"Guys," Flora cut in. "I'm sorry, but this argument is ridiculous. Maybe Jonah had something to do with it, maybe not, but either way there was a skeleton in the attic of my new house and I'm sort of freaking out over here. A *skeleton*." She paused for emphasis. "In a box. In my attic. Why does this keep happening to me?"

While Wade muttered something about her being cursed, Grady came around the counter and pulled her into a hug. "Maybe there's a silver lining," he said. "You're helping that woman get the justice she deserves. If it wasn't for you, her body might not have been found for another decade."

She sniffed, resting her forehead against his chest. "I guess. It was horrible, Grady. I'm never going into an attic alone again. It was like something straight out of a horror movie."

"I'm sorry," he said. "I wish I had been there with you."

She just sniffed again, because she selfishly wished he was there too, even though she knew she should be glad he wasn't. At least this way, she was the only one traumatized by the skeleton in the box. Well, other than Officer Hendricks and Stephen and whoever else ended up investigating the murder. But at least *they* knew to expect it.

"Are you still going to try to flip the house?" he asked her. "Maybe you could just mow the lawn and touch up some paint and sell it for what your bought it for."

"No, I'm not ready to give up," she said, pulling away from him so she could wipe at her eyes. "I'm not in any rush to right now, though. I'll give the police space to do whatever they need to do, and I guess in the meantime, I'll make a list of what all needs to be done." She didn't bother holding back her shiver this time. "Starting with hiring someone to clean out the attic, because I'm sure not doing it myself."

CHAPTER FIVE

Wade had to leave a few minutes later. The spreadsheet he and Grady had been looking over when Flora came in was a record of his income from the scrap hauling business he was trying to start up. He had an appointment at the bank to apply for a business loan. She wished him luck, then slumped against the counter when he was gone.

"Hopefully he has a better day than I've had," she muttered.

"I think he's got a good chance of getting the loan," Grady said. "Are you hungry? We could order a pizza. Ellison is supposed to be here in about an hour; we could ask him to stop and grab some coffees from Violet Delights."

She knew he was trying to cheer her up, but none

of that sounded appetizing right now. She really wasn't in a great mood, and she didn't want to bring him down, so she straightened up, took a deep breath, and said, "Thanks, but I should probably head home." Her skin was still crawling from finding the skeleton in the attic, but she was feeling a little better than she had on her drive here. "I might not be able to start work on the house as soon as I had planned, but I still need to start price shopping and draw up a to-do list. Do you want to come over tonight?"

"Sure," he said. "I'll pick up some food on my way over. Just let me know what you want."

She gave him a quick kiss goodbye and let herself out of the hardware store. She was tempted to swing by the coffee shop, not to order a latte, but to tell Violet what had happened. That sort of conversation wasn't something she wanted to have in public, though. She would call Violet later, after she had closed the coffee shop for the day, and give her the full story then.

Despite everything, she felt a surge of joy in her chest when she pulled into her driveway and parked in front of her house. Just a couple of months ago, she had been on the verge of tears at the thought of selling the place, but an unexpected gift from her Aunt Olivia had put those fears to rest. The house was well and truly hers, and she didn't have the loan from her aunt hanging over her head anymore either. From here on out, she would make it or break it under her own gumption. It was a frightening but exhilarating thought.

Her fluffy white Persian cat, Amaretto, was peering through the living room window, but as soon as she saw Flora getting out of the truck, she vanished. Flora knew she would be waiting by the front door to slip outside, so she ducked to catch the cat as soon as she pushed the front door open. Gently admonishing the squirming feline, she stepped into her house, shoved the door shut behind her, then set the cat down. She stroked down Amaretto's spine before taking her shoes off and hanging her purse on a hook by the door.

"Oh, don't look so sad," Flora said when Amaretto sat right next to the door, her tail flicking back and forth as she looked up at Flora with her large, yellow eyes. "We went on a walk this morning. I'll take you out later if you want, and we can go down to the pond. I need some time to sit and think right now, though."

She walked down the hall to grab her laptop from the kitchen table, then carried it to the living room, where she set it down on the coffee table. Amaretto jumped up onto the couch beside her and settled down in her favorite spot on the back cushion, where she could look out the window onto the porch.

Flora felt bad about keeping her cat indoors when she so obviously wanted to spend time outside, but the Persian had grown up in an apartment. She had long, cotton-like fur that got tangled if Flora looked at it funny, a slightly smushed in face, and absolutely no survival skills. She would never forgive herself if she let Amaretto go outside and the cat got hurt.

An old idea, one that she had dismissed because she was planning on selling the house, came back to her. She narrowed her eyes, looking between the cat and the window. It would take some work and a good number of supplies, but she was pretty sure she could build it herself, though Grady would probably offer to help her.

Amaretto had made it clear the leash walks weren't enough, and Flora wasn't going to bend on letting her cat roam around outside unsupervised, but there was a compromise that might make them both happy. A catio. Since this house was well and truly hers, and she was planning on spending many more years here, she could go all out. She could build a structure that wrapped around the house, with plenty of platforms, climbing posts, and tunnels, so

Amaretto could enjoy the great outdoors behind the safety of sturdy wire, far out of reach of coyotes and speeding cars.

She opened her laptop and logged in, pulling up a blank document where she added *Build a catio for Amaretto* as the first bullet point in her to-do list.

That would be her personal project, something she hoped to get done by the end of summer. She could look up designs later. Right now, she wanted to focus on the house.

The first thing she needed to do was get a quote on the installation of a water tank and a furnace. She noted that down, then pulled up her browser to start looking for local companies. She wouldn't make an appointment just yet – she didn't know how long the police would need her to stay out of the house — but she could at least read some reviews and find a handful of promising companies.

The image of the skeleton in the box flashed in front of her eyes again and she took a deep breath, trying to shove the image away. She hoped the police solved the case quickly. With it being a decade-old cold case, she didn't have her hopes up, but at the same time, the killer almost *had* to be either Jonah or Mason, didn't it? Her body was hidden in Mason Mitchell's house. It made no sense for her to be hidden there if he or his son hadn't been involved in her death.

Maybe whoever had killed her would confess now that her body had been found. After a decade, they must have thought they had gotten away with it.

She frowned. If Mason or Jonah were the killer, why wouldn't they have moved her body prior to selling the house? They had to know there was a good chance either Flora or one of the many other people involved in the sale of a house would find the body tucked away in the attic. It wouldn't have been difficult for them to carry the box out to the woods and hide it somewhere far away from anything that could link her to them.

The only reason she could think of why they wouldn't try to move the body before selling the house was if they didn't know she was up there.

But if that was true, then who had killed Annabelle Morgan?

She wasn't going to be able to focus on putting together a plan to fix up the house until she knew more about the case. Opening a new tab on her internet browser, she typed *Annabelle Morgan missing Warbler Kentucky* in the search bar and clicked on the first link that came up. It led to a webpage dedicated to unsolved mysteries.

Wade had described the case well. After coming back to Warbler to visit her family for the summer during a college break, Annabelle had vanished while going to see her boyfriend one night. Apparently, she had never made it to the Mitchells' house.

Jonah was mentioned in the article as a possible suspect, but the article stated that no arrests had ever been made, though it didn't go into any more detail than that. There was a blurb at the end that caught her eye, a quote from someone named Kaycee Anniston.

"Annabelle was my best friend, and I know it's been years since her disappearance but I still hold out the hope that she's alive. If you're out there some-where, Annabelle, come home. We all miss you."

Beneath it was a photo of two women, standing with their arms linked. The one on the right was Annabelle, her light brown hair pulled back into a ponytail and a cheerful smile on her face. The one on the left was labeled as Kaycee Anniston, her blonde hair in a pixie cut and a pair of goofy, black rimmed glasses perched on her nose.

Flora recognized those glasses and that face. Kaycee Aniston was still in town. She worked at the gas station, and Flora saw her almost every time she stopped to fill up her truck.

CHAPTER SIX

Flora was not going to get involved. She was definitely not going to try to talk to Annabelle's best friend about her disappearance. Even if she wanted to, it wouldn't be right to bring up her friend's murder just to assuage her own curiosity.

Unless…. maybe Kaycee would *want* to talk to Flora. She might be even hungrier for answers than Flora was. If something happened to Violet, Flora didn't think she would ever stop wanting to get to the bottom of it, not even ten years later.

Well, either way, she wasn't going to talk to Kaycee tonight. She needed to let the police do their work while she did hers, which meant it was time for her to focus on making her to-do list and organize her plans for the yellow house.

She was a little surprised when she actually managed to stay on task. She spent the next few hours researching and writing up a long list of everything she wanted to start with on the house to get it livable, then she printed off a few designs she found for catios online and made a list of the supplies she would need for that.

With her work done, she called Violet and spent a good hour on the phone with her, talking about the body and hearing her friend's take on the original disappearance.

When Grady came over that evening, they walked around the outside of the house and took measurements. She might have to work on it here and there in between the more important project of getting the yellow house ready to sell, but one way or the other, Amaretto was going to get her catio before the summer was over. She loved her feline friend and wanted her to be both happy, and safe.

She decided to go in for a shift at the hardware store the next day. She was only *supposed* to be working one shift a week there right now. Grady, Ellison, and Mark were covering the rest of them, since they had planned on her being busy with the new house. With the police investigation keeping her away, it was going to be a while before she could really throw herself into working on it, and she didn't feel good about sitting around at home while Grady and their employees did all of the hard work without her.

She stopped by Violet Delights first to get some iced coffees for her, Grady, and Mark. Violet chatted while she made the drinks, and nodded at a stack of papers that was just behind the counter.

"Annabelle's parents stopped in to ask if I would put some flyers up for them. You can take one if you want, but I'm sure her family stopped by the hardware store too. I agreed to hang them up this afternoon."

"What are they?" Flora asked as she picked up one of the flyers. Her question was answered immediately. A photo of Annabelle was front and center, and the text promised a reward if anyone was able to step forward with information about the case. Even after all these years, Annabelle's family was desperate for answers. The discovery of her body might have taken away any hope of finding her alive, but now they had a renewed hope that they would get to learn the truth about what happened to her.

"I wish I could help," she said. "This must be so hard for them."

"You've given them closure," Violet said. "That's

more than anyone else managed over the last decade. Here, the one on the far left is your white chocolate caramel latte. The other two are the mochas."

Flora took the drink tray Violet handed her with a quiet thanks and said a quick goodbye before hurrying back out to her truck.

Before long, the entire town would know that Annabelle's body had been found, and it probably wouldn't take them long to realize she was the one who had made the discovery. She hoped the case wasn't as well known in the local area as Wade seemed to think, because she really wasn't looking forward to the unwanted infamy that would come when people learned she had found the body.

Sure enough, there was another stack of flyers at the hardware store when she arrived. She passed out the drinks, tossed the drink tray in the garbage, and then picked up one of the flyers, which was identical to the one from the coffee shop.

"Should we start hanging these up?"

"Annabelle's parents asked us to wait until around three this afternoon to put them up. Apparently, there's going to be a press release about her case, and they don't want to field too many questions before that. I figured we'd put some up in the window and leave the rest on the counter for customers to take."

"Did they stop at every business on Main Street? There were a bunch at the coffee shop as well."

He shrugged. "I think so. This is going to be big, Flora. If you want me to stay with you for a few days, I'm more than happy to."

She bit her lip, looking outside. It was a sunny day, but there was a looming sense of a storm brewing, nonetheless. "Maybe. Let's just wait and see. The police said they were going to try to keep my name out of it."

"Someone's going to realize you just bought the house where her body was hidden and put two and two together," he said.

She winced, because he was right. If a reporter showed up and started knocking on doors, Wyatt Cooper would be able to tell them exactly who she was. He had no reason to keep her name out of it. She would just have to deal with the publicity when it came.

"Before I forget, Wade wanted me to ask you to call him."

She blinked and refocused on the conversation at hand. "Really? What does he want?"

"I have no idea," Grady said. "If I had to guess, I'd say it's probably got something to do with Annabelle. He called me this morning to tell me he managed to get his loan, but he barely seemed to care about it. I think this case is really bothering him."

"Oh, he got the loan? That's good. I'll have to congratulate him."

Grady handed her his phone so she could get Wade's number out of it, then she stepped into the back room to call him. She had no idea what he wanted to talk about, but if it did have something to do with Annabelle, it probably wasn't a conversation she wanted to have around Mark and their customers.

"Yeah?" Wade grunted when he answered.

"Hi, it's Flora. Grady said you wanted to talk to me?"

"Oh, good, I wasn't sure when I'd hear from you. Listen, do you want to help me with something?"

"That depends on what it is," she said warily. He might not have committed the crime that got him sent to prison, but he was still known as a troublemaker for a good reason.

"I want to figure out what happened to Annabelle. I know you've got a little experience figuring this sort of thing out. I figured if we work together, we might actually be able to do some good. What do you say, do you want to help me do some digging? We can bring Grady in too, of course, but I think he's more likely to say yes if you've already agreed."

Flora hesitated, but hadn't she just been wishing she could do something to help?

"As long as it doesn't interfere with the police investigation, I'm in," she said at last. "Actually, I've already got some ideas. I think we should start by seeing if her best friend will talk to us. A woman named Kaycee Anniston. She works at the gas station on the corner of East and Green."

"I'm taking a break for lunch in about two hours. Want to meet there? She'll be more likely to talk to you than me, but I want to hear what she has to say."

It wasn't as if she was actually on the schedule today, and she knew Grady and Mark had things covered without her. If she and Wade could actually make a difference, then this was probably a better use of her time. "Sure. I'll be there at noon."

CHAPTER SEVEN

She still wasn't sure if talking to Kaycee was the right thing to do or not, but she figured she and Wade could feel it out. When she returned to the front of the store, she told Grady what she and his brother were planning on doing. He looked a little exasperated by Wade, but said, "Just be careful. I understand why you both feel so invested in this case, but I don't want you to get hurt."

"We're not going to do anything dangerous," she said. "I just want to know more about what happened back when she first disappeared. Besides, sooner or later, my name is going to get out. I'm already involved whether I want to be or not, and at least this way, I've got someone else along for the ride. You're welcome to come too, if you want."

"Nah. I'm glad the two of you are bonding. But Wade better know if he gets you hurt, I won't forgive him."

She pressed a kiss to his cheek and grabbed the store's daily checklist. She had a couple hours before she had to leave to meet Wade, and she wanted to pull her weight while she was here instead of just lingering around Grady and chatting.

"I can take care of myself, and we'll both be fine. Let's get to work. Oh, and I need to buy some of the supplies for the catio before I head out today. Thank goodness I bought a pickup truck. I don't know how I ever survived without one."

She supposed she simply hadn't needed one before. She barely drove back when she lived in Chicago, and she certainly hadn't needed to transport anything too large to fit in the trunk of her car on a regular basis. Sometimes it still surprised her just how much her lifestyle had changed. She did a lot more physical work now, her paychecks were a little less reliable, and she had to be a lot more independent, but she was also so much happier here in Warbler than she had ever been with her nice apartment and her desk job in Chicago. She thought getting some country air and learning some new skills was part of it, but her friends and Grady were another big part of why she was so happy now. Home was where the heart was, and her heart was here.

She left just before noon, with lengths of lumber and rolls of wire tied down in the bed of her truck. The gas station was only a couple of blocks away, and since she was almost down to a quarter of a tank of gas, she pulled up to a pump. The rusty old car Wade had bought over the winter was parked in one of the spaces by the door, and she could see him sitting in the driver's seat. She memorized the number of the pump she was at and got out of the truck, walking across the parking lot toward him. As soon as he noticed her, he got out of his car.

"What are you building?" he asked, eyeing the pieces of wood that were sticking out of the back of her truck.

"I'm building a catio for my cat," she said as they went inside.

"A what, now?"

"It's an enclosed area attached to one of my windows so my cat can go outside without being in danger or being free to kill a bunch of birds and squirrels," she told him.

"Huh." He looked puzzled, but didn't say anything more, just looked around the gas station then nudged her, nodding toward the woman behind the counter.

"Is that her?" he asked quietly.

She nodded. Kaycee Anniston. She hadn't known the woman's name before, but she was here almost every time Flora stopped for gas. She wasn't sure if she owned the gas station or was just an employee, but she wasn't surprised to find her behind the counter today.

"Let me do the talking," she muttered to Wade as they approached. "I want to see how she's doing. She may not have even heard yet, and I don't want to upset her."

He nodded and fell back until he was a step behind her. Flora took her wallet out of her purse as she approached the counter. Kaycee gave her a weak smile. Her eyes were red, as if she had been crying. Her hair was still blonde and still in a pixie bob cut, but the thick-rimmed glasses had been replaced with a thinner, sparkling pink frame.

"Good afternoon. How can I help you?"

"Can I get fifty dollars on pump four?" Flora asked. She passed her card over, and she decided to take a chance. "Are you all right?"

Kaycee grimaced. "It's that obvious, is it? Sorry, I'm a mess today. You're new to town, so you might not know this, but a decade ago, a woman went missing here in Warbler. Well, the woman who disappeared was one of my best friends, and I just got the news this morning that they found her body. A mutual friend stopped in to tell me, and I haven't been able to stop crying since."

Flora immediately regretted coming here. It was obvious Kaycee was grieving, and she didn't want to make things worse for the other woman. Still, she felt that she owed her the truth. She would probably learn Flora had found her friend's body eventually, and she didn't want to keep the truth from her right now. It felt too much like lying.

"I did hear about that, actually. I'm… well, I'm the one who found her. If you ever want to talk about it, just let me know. I can leave you my number."

Kaycee turned to her, her eyes wide with shock. Flora's debit card slipped from her fingers and clattered to the counter. "*You* found her body? Where? When? Do you know what happened to her? No one's telling me anything, Jonah just told me someone found her body and the news would probably say something about it later today."

She hadn't expected Kaycee to be quite so enthusiastic about talking to her, but she could hardly look a gift horse in the mouth.

"Well, it sounds like you know Jonah. Do you know his father?" she asked. "He owned a little yellow house not far from here. I bought it the other day, and I found her while I was exploring the attic."

Kaycee's lips pulled down in a tight frown. "You found her body in Jonah's old house? He didn't say anything about that, he just said the body had been found. Hidden in his own house…" She shivered. "But surely the police would have arrested him by now if he did something to her."

"Considering where I found her body, I would be shocked if he and his father weren't major suspects," Flora said. "They probably don't want to move too fast until they have enough evidence to back up any charges. Do you know if there were ever any suspects other than Jonah?"

"Not officially, unless her family knew something and didn't tell me about it." She hesitated and glanced around to make sure the store was still empty except for them, then leaned over the counter. "I'm not saying I think there's no way Jonah killed her, not anymore — not if she was hidden in his childhood home — but he seemed a little too normal and nice to do something like that." Behind Flora, Wade made a triumphant sound, and she elbowed him without looking at him. "I always thought it was more likely that creepy neighbor of theirs did something to her. We all grew up here — you know how it is in small towns — and Annabelle and I were friends with Jonah for a long time before she started dating him. We used to go over to his house to play video games, and their creepy neighbor was always watching us. Annabelle never felt comfortable around him and neither did I." She leaned back and sighed. "But maybe it *was* Jonah. I mean, it almost has to have been him or his dad, doesn't it?"

"He doesn't have any siblings?" Wade asked. "No mother in the picture?"

Kaycee shook her head. "It was just the two of them. His mom passed away when he was in middle school. He never had any brothers or sisters. But like I said, Jonah is an average, normal guy, and I don't see why his father would have killed her and hidden her body away for a decade. Besides, the police must have investigated them both already, since he was dating her when she vanished. They must have had a reason to think he wasn't guilty."

"Maybe, or maybe they just didn't have enough evidence to charge him with anything," Flora said.

"Well, if you hear anything more about it, will you tell me? Annabelle was like a sister to me. I just want to know what happened to her."

"I will," Flora said. "I really hope you get the answers you deserve, and her family, too."

Kaycee printed out her receipt and handed that and her debit card over, then they exchanged numbers. She didn't feel like she was any closer to figuring out who Annabelle's killer was, but she did know a lot more about the original case. A decade was such a long time. It seemed almost impossible to hope that there was still evidence to find after so many years.

CHAPTER EIGHT

While Wade bought a prepackaged sandwich and some soda for himself for lunch, she filled her tank. He came out before she finished.

"See? I told you. She knows Jonah a lot better than me and even she agrees he isn't the killing type."

"I'm not saying you're wrong," she said. "I barely know any of these people. But *someone* killed Annabelle, and I found her in the Mitchells' boarded up attic. The killer almost *has* to have been Jonah or his dad, and I don't know why Mason Mitchell would kill his son's girlfriend."

"Well, how about we go talk to that other guy she mentioned? Maybe he still lives near them."

"He does," Flora said with a sigh. "I met him yesterday. He lives right across the street. I didn't get any creepy vibes from him, but I only met him the once."

"So, let's go chat with him," Wade said. "To *me,* it sounds like he's the most likely suspect."

She pressed her lips together. It was true that the house had been sitting empty for years, and she knew there had been at least a few break-ins. It was possible Wyatt had hidden her body there after the Mitchells moved out… or maybe even while they were living there, if they went out of town and he knew where their key was hidden.

"I'm not sure," she said as she returned the nozzle to the pump and screwed her gas cap on. "I might not be planning on living at that house, but I'm still going to see an awful lot of Wyatt and his wife. I don't want to get off on the wrong foot with them. And if you're right, and he's behind this, he might decide you and I should be his next victims. I don't want to have to look over my shoulder every time I'm at the house."

"Aren't you going to be looking over your shoulder anyway?" Wade asked. "The way I see it is you and I are both already involved in this. It might have been a while since I worked for Mr. Morgan, but I remember everything about her disappearance, especially those first few weeks. I always hoped she'd be found, and now that she has been, I want to know exactly what happened to her. I thought you of all people would understand that. You're always getting involved in little mysteries, and you helped me before, back when I first got back to town."

"I do understand," she told him. "And you're right that I'm going to be looking over my shoulder until this is solved either way. I'll go with you to talk to Wyatt, but let me do the talking again, all right? Don't accuse him of anything. I really don't want to start off on the wrong foot with this guy."

"Hey, I won't say a word if you don't want me to. Do you want to drive together? My car is kind of a beater."

"Yeah, hop in," Flora said.

She had driven past the yellow house enough in the months leading up to the sale that she could probably have driven to it in her sleep, from anywhere in Warbler. She slowed as she turned onto the correct block and pulled up along the curb in front of the house. There was crime scene tape across the front door, and she spent a long moment just staring at it.

"It's a nice place," Wade said, breaking the silence.

She snorted. "It's a wreck. But it's going to be nice."

"I believe you," he said as he unbuckled his seatbelt. "Grady showed me the before and after pictures of your other house. You'll get this place fixed up in no time."

"Hopefully it's not hiding anymore nasty surprises," she muttered as she opened her door and stepped out of the truck.

Tearing her attention away from her new house, she looked across the street at Wyatt's house. He really did have a lot of garden gnomes. They were charming before, but now that she knew he might be a cold-blooded killer, they seemed a lot creepier.

She didn't see Wyatt, but a woman was gardening in the front flowerbeds, her long, graying hair held back with a headband. She looked up as Flora and Wade crossed the street, shading her eyes against the sun before rising to her feet.

"Hello, there," she called out. "Are you the couple who bought the old Mitchell house?"

"We're not a couple," Wade said, sputtering.

"I'm dating his brother," Flora explained. "I *am* the one who bought the house, though. Are you Willow? I think I spoke to your husband yesterday."

"That's me," Willow said, giving them a kind smile. She pulled off her gardening gloves to shake Flora's hand. "It's so nice to meet you. I'm glad that house got sold to someone who knows how to fix it up. It was so nice just a few years ago, but after Mason had to go into assisted living, it just fell apart. Jonah has his own place, and I guess he just couldn't keep up with both of them. What can I help the two of you with?"

"Have you heard about Annabelle Morgan?" Flora asked.

Willow nodded, her smile turning into a somber frown. "We spoke to the police yesterday, after you made that horrible discovery. Just the thought of that poor woman's body being hidden across the street from us all those years makes me shiver. I'm so sorry you had to be the one to find her."

"I have got a lot of questions about what happened back when she disappeared," Flora said. "I've only lived in Warbler for about two and a half years. I hate to bother you about this, but you wouldn't happen to know anything about the original case, would you?"

"As a matter of fact, we do. Wyatt and I watched it all unfold. If anyone deserves to know, it's you, considering the house you just bought. Why don't you and your friend come on in?"

Flora hesitated but Wade was with her, and he didn't look at all worried, so after a moment's pause, they followed Willow inside. A TV was on in the other room with the volume up, but Willow called out, "Wyatt, guests! They're here to talk about Annabelle!" and the sound muted immediately. Wyatt came out of the room a moment later, giving Flora and Wade a surprised greeting.

Soon, they were ensconced in the Coopers' kitchen. It was a cute, if cluttered, kitchen with an out-of-control house plant growing over the fridge, and lots of little figurines on the counters and shelves. Willow poured them some tea and Wade eyed his skeptically until she put a tray with sugar cubes and cream in the center of the table.

"We're talking about a murder, Willow, not having a tea party," Wyatt grumbled, but he poured himself a cup too. "So, you've got questions about what happened to Annabelle?"

Flora nodded. "We talked to a friend of hers earlier today, a woman named Kaycee Anniston, and she mentioned that you lived here back when Annabelle disappeared. I'm just wondering what happened, exactly. Does anyone know the circum-stances of her disappearance?"

Wyatt snorted. "Kaycee Anniston. I haven't heard *that* name in years. Oh, boy. And she said she was a friend of Annabelle's?"

At his shoulder, Willow tittered, covering her lips

politely. Flora exchanged a puzzled look with Wade, then looked over at Wyatt again.

"Yes? Were they not friends?"

"Oh, no," Wyatt said. "Maybe they started out that way, but those two girls hated each other." He leaned forward a little, as if sharing a secret. "I retired early, you see. An old injury to my knee made it so I couldn't keep up with the job anymore. Now, before Willow got me into all my hobbies, I used to spend a lot of time just people watching from the porch. And let me tell you, I saw a lot going on at that Mitchell house."

"Like what?"

"I'm sure you heard Annabelle was dating Mason's son, Jonah. What you might not know was that Jonah Mitchell and Kaycee Anniston were seeing each other, too. I started to see her coming over when Annabelle left for college, but they kept it up even when she came back for her summer breaks, they were just sneakier about it. After dark, she'd climb right up that trellis on the side of the house and through his window, and it was obvious they were trying to keep it a secret. I think Annabelle figured it out, because I heard the two of them get into a screaming match while they were both visiting him at the same time one day. Kaycee was the one who got the boot, and Annabelle kept coming around, so I guess she was more forgiving than Willow would be if I ever got myself into the same mess."

"Darn right," Willow said, patting his shoulder. "And don't you forget it."

"Wow. I mean, thanks for telling us," Flora said. "I had no idea."

He nodded, then glanced at his wife, who cleared her throat. "Back when she first disappeared, we both thought she might have just left town to go back to her university early without telling anyone. I personally figured she finally ended things with Jonah and didn't want to waste her time here anymore. I think that's what most people thought, but it was Jonah who kept insisting everything was wrong. He went door to door even before the police picked up the investigation, asking if anyone had seen her. Looking back, I wonder if he felt guilty, and was trying his best to hide it."

"I used to work for her father, so I knew them a little," Wade interjected. "Do you really think Jonah could do something like that?"

Wade crossed his arms. "If there's one thing I've learned after all these years, it's that love and hate can both make people do crazy things, especially when the love and hate are both directed at the same person.

I don't want to say I think Jonah killed her, because I don't know for certain either way, but I can tell you that not a soul in this town believes it was a stranger who killed her. Whoever did it was someone who knew her, and the two people who had the most motive for it are Kaycee Anniston and Jonah Mitchell. Nothing good ever came out of a love triangle."

CHAPTER NINE

Everyone she talked to seemed to point their fingers at someone else. She wasn't sure what she had expected. If anyone had any useful information, they would have given it to the police years ago.

She knew she should be grateful that they were even willing to talk to her, so although she wanted to sigh in frustration, she opened her mouth to thank Wyatt and Willow. Before she got the chance, Willow walked over to the kitchen window with a frown.

"Are you expecting company, Flora?"

"No. Why?"

"Someone just pulled into your driveway."

It still felt strange to think of the yellow house as *hers*, so it took her a moment to realize Willow wasn't talking about the farmhouse. She stood up and hurried over to the window, standing next to Willow as she peered through the glass. Sure enough, a tan sedan was parked in her driveway. She had a feeling she had seen the vehicle before, but she couldn't quite place it.

"Is it the police?" Wade asked from behind her.

"No," she said, turning away from the window to look at their hosts. "I don't know who it is, but I'd better go find out. Thanks for taking the time to talk to us. I appreciate it."

"Anytime," Willow said, just as her husband said, "You might not be planning to live there, but as far as I'm concerned, you're still a neighbor."

She gave them a quick, grateful smile, and hurried back to the front door, Wade tagging along behind her. After pushing through the door and rushing past the garden gnomes, she paused to check both ways, then crossed the street. She could see someone at the front door, standing in front of the crime scene tape. As soon as her feet hit the sidewalk, she called out to them.

"Hello? How can I help you?"

When the person at her front door turned around, she finally recognized him. Jonah. That was why the sedan looked so familiar – she had seen it when he picked his father up from the title company.

"Oh, hi. You're the new owner, right?" he asked, looking her up and down. His eyes flicked back to Wade, then he refocused on her. "I'm looking for my father. You haven't seen him, have you?"

"I haven't," Flora said. "Why would he be here?"

"He has issues with his memory," Jonah explained, his shoulder slumping. "He lives in an assisted living apartment on the other side of Main Street, but every once in a while he gets confused and leaves without telling anyone. He usually ends up going somewhere familiar. I got a call about half an hour ago saying they couldn't find him, so I thought I would check here."

"Well, I haven't seen him," Flora told him gently. "He seemed fine when I saw him at the title company the other day."

"That's what makes it so hard," Jonah said. "He is fine, until he's not. He'll get confused and think he's in the 1980s and is still working at the factory. Or he'll confuse me with his brother, who passed away twenty years ago. He usually snaps out of it pretty quickly, but it worries me every time."

"What does he look like?" Wade asked. "There's a lot of old men in town, and I've never met the guy."

Jonah described his father for Wade's benefit, then added, "I don't want to scare you. He's perfectly harmless, and he doesn't have these episodes very often. If he ever does show up here, he might think he still lives here. Just explain what's going on, and give me a call. Here, I'll give you my number. I should have done it when I saw you at the title company, but he's sensitive about this and I didn't want to embarrass him."

Flora traded phones with him so they could each enter their contact information. As she handed his phone back and accepted hers, she said, "I'll call you right away if I see him." She hesitated, fighting the urge to ask about Annabelle's body. His eyes met hers, and for a moment, she was absolutely certain he was thinking about Annabelle too.

Was he really here to look for his father, or was he trying to get into the house for some reason? Maybe there was evidence in the house he wanted to cover up, or another body he wanted to move.

Then he looked away and the moment passed. Instead of bringing up Annabelle's name, she just smiled at him politely and said, "I hope you find him soon."

"Thanks, so do I. I'd better get going. Sorry again for disturbing you."

She shifted to let him walk past her, then she and Wade turned to watch him climb into his car and back out of the driveway.

"See what I mean? He's way too normal to be a murderer," Wade muttered once he had pulled away.

Flora just shook her head, leading the way back to her truck. "I don't trust him. Let's go back to the hardware store and tell Grady everything we found out."

"It doesn't feel like we did much," he complained as he got the passenger seat. "And don't forget, we need to pick up my car first."

"Right. And no, it doesn't, but I can't think of anything else to do right now, and we did learn *some* things. Namely, that none of these people actually got along very well."

He chuckled as she pulled away from the curb. "It's a small town. To half of these people, their best friend is also their worst enemy, depending on the day of the week. Nah, we didn't learn anything worth our while."

Choosing not to believe him, she hit her blinker and turned toward the hardware store. There had to be something they were missing, something that would solve this decade-old case once and for all.

Logic told her Jonah was still the most likely

suspect. She knew in her heart that Wade was wrong, that his seemingly normal persona didn't mean a thing. The most dangerous people were the ones who could commit atrocities and pretend nothing was wrong. Just because Jonah acted normal, didn't mean he was innocent.

When Flora and Wade arrived at the hardware store, Mark and Grady were busy mopping the floors, but they stopped to listen to Wade tell them about their amateur attempt at an investigation in great detail. Flora made sure to remind everyone not to spread any of this around — Annabelle's disappearance and murder was a mystery to be solved to them, but to her family and friends, it was a very personal tragedy. She hoped they could trust Mark not to gossip; she didn't know him very well yet, but she didn't have the heart to exclude him when the rest of them were talking together.

By the time they finished hypothesizing with each other, it was after three, and Violet called to ask if Flora is busy that evening. Somehow, in the course of a short conversation, a girls' night in morphed into a cookout with both of their boyfriends and Wade, since he was standing right there and it would have been rude for her to invite Grady and not him.

The unexpected cookout meant that she had to go grocery shopping and get home early enough to tidy her house before her guests arrived. The day was an odd mix of busy and oddly pointless; she didn't get anything done – she didn't even get started on the catio – but she somehow barely had the chance to sit down until the cookout was in full swing and she had a burger on a paper plate in her hands and a fire flickering in the fire pit in her back yard.

"Ooh, I know what your next project should be," Violet said as she tried to press the top of her bun down over the ridiculous number of toppings she had put on her burger. "You should build one of those enclosed fire pits next to the pavilion down by the pond. That way, we can sit out there and have a fire without having to worry about a spark catching on the trees. You could even make one of those floating platforms for the water. It would be perfect for summer nights like this."

"That's a good idea, but I need to focus on the new house for a while first," Flora said. "I really want to get a good start on the renovations. There is so much to do, I'm going to start getting stressed if I don't make progress soon."

"What about that cat pen thing you were talking

about earlier?" Wade chimed in from across the fire. She felt a little bad for him, since he was a fifth wheel. Maybe she and Grady could start subtly matchmaking him with a few of the women they knew.

"The catio? Yeah, I'm going to be working on that too, but it's going to take a while. It's for Amaretto, not me."

"Do you know yet when you'll be able to access the house again?" Sydney asked. "I haven't even seen it yet."

"I'll give you all a tour once the police say I can go back," she said. "I'll call Officer Hendricks in the morning and ask him how much longer it will be."

"Do you think the fact that a body was hidden there is going to impact how much you're able to sell the house for?" Violet asked.

Flora frowned. She hadn't considered that. "Maybe. I'll probably have to disclose it, at least. If the police don't end up solving the case by the time I'm ready to sell it, I might have trouble finding a buyer."

She wasn't sure *she* would want to knowingly buy a house with a decade-old cold case attached to it.

Violet's concern was a valid one, though she wished her friend hadn't brought it up right when she was starting to relax. Now she wanted to solve Annabelle's murder even more – both for the sake of the woman whose life ended long before it should have, and for her own sake, so she could sell the little yellow house for a tidy profit and use the money to start progressing in her house flipping career.

CHAPTER TEN

Flora was woken up the next morning by an unhappy cat yowling pitifully by the bedroom door. A glance at the clock on her bedside table told her why Amaretto was being so dramatic – it was just past nine, and she was hungry.

After lingering in bed for a few more moments for a luxurious stretch, she grabbed her phone and shuffled barefoot down the stairs and into the kitchen, where she emptied a can of Amaretto's favorite food into her bowl, hit the button to turn the coffee maker on, and stumbled into the bathroom to freshen up.

She was not and would never be a morning person. As soon as she looked and felt a little less like something the cat had dragged in, she returned to the kitchen and poured herself a hot cup of coffee. After adding the correct amounts of cream and sugar – she had no idea what the actual measurements were, it was all just instinct by now – she sat down at the kitchen table and picked up her phone to scroll mindlessly through social media until the caffeine hit her bloodstream and she was awake enough to do something worthwhile.

There was a text message waiting for her on her phone. She blinked at the name *Kaycee* for a moment until she remembered exchanging numbers with Kaycee Anniston at the gas station. Wondering why the woman had messaged her – sure, she had offered, but she hadn't actually expected to hear from her – she tapped on the message to open it.

Hi, this is Kaycee. When we talked about Annabelle, you said if there was anything else I wanted to talk to you about, I could contact you. I hope you meant that, because I really need to talk to someone. I need to get this off my chest. Could we meet somewhere to talk privately this morning?

Kaycee had sent the message at seven-thirty, and Flora felt a little bad about not seeing it until now. She was about to respond but hesitated before her fingers typed out her answer. Her initial reaction was to agree to meet Kaycee somewhere, but was that smart? It was possible she had been involved in

Annabelle's death, especially if what Wyatt said was true.

She was tempted to see if Wade or Grady would go with her when she met Kaycee, but she had a feeling bringing someone else along would make the other woman less willing to talk, and she really did want to hear what she had to say.

Meeting somewhere to talk privately didn't have to mean meeting somewhere isolated. She responded with an offer to meet at Violet Delights at ten — there was no way she was going to be ready for the day before then — then sent a screenshot of the conversation to the group message she shared with Violet, Grady, and Sydney. If she disappeared like Annabelle had, at least someone would know who to blame.

Kaycee sent a message to confirm the meeting just a few minutes later. Flora was out of the shower by nine-forty and on the road by nine-fifty. While she drove, she sent a call to Officer Hendricks through her truck's bluetooth connection. It had been a couple of days since she found the body, and she was itching to finally start working on the house.

"I am not at all surprised to be hearing from you, Ms. Abner. Did something else happen, or are you checking up on your new house?"

"Thankfully, the latter. I'm not trying to rush you

guys, but do you know when I'll be able to have the house to myself again?"

"Give us one more day. We'll be out of your hair by Saturday morning. Is that good enough?"

"That's perfect. Thank you. There won't be any issues if I hire cleaners, will there?"

"There shouldn't be. We've gone through the entire property with a fine-toothed comb. If you or anyone you hire to work there does find something that seems connected with the case, please contact the police station immediately, but I would be shocked if you managed to find something my men couldn't."

She bit back a mean-spirited retort that she had managed to find an *entire body* when they couldn't. That wasn't their fault. She knew the police had to follow regulations and a lot of red tape. They couldn't just go snooping through someone's house without a warrant, and they couldn't get a warrant without evidence.

"Well, thanks for taking my call and thanks for telling me when I can get to work on the house. Have you made any progress on the case yet?"

"Nothing that we have shared with the public," he said.

It was a non-answer, but she would have been more surprised if he had said something else. They might be sort-of-friends, but that didn't mean he was going to go against policy and give her confidential information. It had been worth a try, though.

She thanked him again and ended the call, feeling a little better at the knowledge that she would be able to start work on the house this coming weekend. Now that she had a solid date to work off of, she could start calling around to get quotes for a furnace and water heater installation.

Thoughts of the upcoming renovation were on her mind when she pulled up to the coffee shop. She had no idea what vehicle Kaycee drove, so she just went inside. Violet waved to her from behind the counter, and Flora gave a distracted wave back as she looked around. She spotted Kaycee in the corner. The other woman already had a drink with her, so Flora went up to the counter and ordered her usual latte.

"I got your message," Violet said casually as she made the drink. "Let me know if you need anything."

"I will," Flora said. "Thanks."

It was Violet's way of letting her know she would be keeping an eye on things. Shooting a grateful smile at her friend, she carried her drink over to join Kaycee at the table.

"This isn't as private as I was hoping," Kaycee

said, looking around. "But thanks for meeting me here."

"I was surprised to hear from you," Flora admitted. "What did you want to talk about?"

The other woman took a deep breath. "Well, with the discovery of Annabelle's body, it's been like I'm reliving the first weeks after she disappeared. There's something I told the police about, but no one else, and with how the public sentiment is turning out, I'm beginning to think I need to come clean."

"What is it?"

"Jonah was dating Annabelle, but he was seeing me on the side." She squeezed her eyes shut, bowing her head. "Annabelle was my best friend, or she used to be, but when she found out, she stopped talking to me completely. Jonah and I stopped seeing each other for a while, and when we started up again, we were a lot more secretive about when and where we met. I'm only telling you all of this because of some rumors I've been hearing. People tried to blame Jonah for her disappearance the last time around, and now they're blaming him for her murder." She raised her head to meet Flora's eyes. "But I know for a fact he didn't kill her, because he was with me the night she disappeared."

CHAPTER ELEVEN

"Why are you telling me this?" Flora asked.

Kaycee considered her for a moment, her eyebrows drawing together. "You don't seem surprised. You already knew, didn't you?"

"I've been trying to figure out what happened to Annabelle," Flora admitted. "I'm just not sure why you're telling *me*, of all people, about this."

"Have you seen what people are saying online? I've seen so many nasty comments about Jonah. There are people out there who are certain he killed her, but *I* know he couldn't have, because he was with me all night. My testimony is probably the only thing that kept him from getting arrested back when she first disappeared. We haven't spoken for years, but I hate watching people blame him for something so horrible, especially when I know for a fact that he's innocent. I just… I don't know how to do it. I don't know what people are going to think of me. You're not connected to any of this, not really. You're an outsider, so I guess it's a little easier to ask you for advice than someone I actually know. What do you think I should do?"

"I don't know," Flora said. She wasn't sure what she had been expecting when Kaycee asked her to meet, but it definitely wasn't this. "Maybe you could start by talking to people who know both of you? Tell them you were with him that night, so you know he didn't have anything to do with what happened to Annabelle. At least that would help him with the people he knows personally."

"People are going to start dragging me into it, though. I don't want to be involved in this! What would you do, if you were in my shoes?"

I wouldn't be *in your shoes,* Flora thought, but she kept that to herself. She would never approve of cheating in relationships, but it was a decade in the past and false accusations of murder were on another level entirely. There were lives that could still be wrecked by all of this. "If I had a friend who was being accused of something they didn't do, I would defend them," she said firmly. "I think you just have to do whatever you think is right."

Kaycee slumped, but nodded reluctantly. "Thanks, I guess. Sorry I dragged you all the way out here for this."

"It's all right. I did say I'd be happy to talk to you if you needed it."

She didn't regret meeting Kaycee, but she was glad when she could make her excuses and leave. It was with a sense of relief that she headed to the hardware store for another midday shift.

She let herself in through the employee entrance this time, and found Grady in the garden center, stacking bags of mulch. He straightened up and brushed his hands off when he saw her.

"Is Wade planning on stopping by today?" she asked after greeting him with a kiss.

He raised an eyebrow, looking amused. "You spent one day hanging out with him, and you're already best buds?"

She wrinkled her nose. "Hardly. But I did agree to help him figure out what happened to Annabelle, and I just had the weirdest meeting with Kaycee Anniston…"

Resigning herself to repeating the story whenever

she saw Wade, she told Grady about her unexpected coffee date with the other woman.

"I bet Wade is going to be happy to hear that," he said. "He really didn't think Jonah did it."

"I have to admit, after hearing Kaycee out, I have to agree with him. Unless she was lying."

"Did you get the feeling she was lying?"

Flora sighed. "Honestly? This is all so tangled up, I don't know what to think."

She busied herself with work, and spent a pleasant day with Grady at the hardware store. After work, they ordered a couple of pizzas and went across the street to Grady's apartment for dinner, where Wade met them and she got a chance to tell him about her meeting with Kaycee. He was just as smug as she expected about the evidence that Jonah was innocent, though he seemed as frustrated as she was that they weren't any closer to figuring out who the killer was.

Although she was still invested in the case, she was getting more and more excited to finally have her little yellow house back. After promising to pick Grady up at eight the next morning, she left him and Wade to watch some sports game together and went home.

She wasn't an early riser, but she was going to make an exception tomorrow morning.

When she picked Grady up the next day, she was armed with freshly made coffee from Violet Delights and all of the power tools she would need to finish tearing apart the kitchen at the new house.

The little yellow house was just as she left it, minus some trampled grass. Someone – probably Officer Hendricks – had even been kind enough to remove the crime scene tape from the door. She parked in the driveway and unloaded her power tools from the bed of the truck before carrying them inside with Grady. Her excitement flagged a little when she was reminded just how bad the interior of the house was, but she kept up a brave face as they set the power tools down in the living room.

"It's not much yet, but try to envision what it will look like when I'm done with it," she said, leading him through the rooms. When they reached the upstairs bedroom with the attic in it, she let him go up without her. She knew it was ridiculous to be afraid of an empty room in her own house, but she just couldn't bring herself to venture up that rickety wooden ladder again. Not yet.

"It's empty," he told her when he came down. "Are you going to be all right working on this place?"

She took a deep breath and nodded. "I'll have to be," she said firmly.

He gave her hand a tight squeeze, silently telling her he believed in her. "Have you checked out the garage yet?"

Her mood lightened at the reminder. "I haven't – it was locked before, and the real estate agent didn't have the key."

When they got back outside and made their way over to the detached garage, it was evident that the police had forced the sliding door open to search the interior, but it was too heavy for them to lift by themselves. There were barn doors on the side that were held shut with a rusty chain, which looked a little more promising.

"Do you have bolt cutters?" Grady asked.

"Not big enough for this," she said.

"I can run back to the hardware store and grab some," he said. "Do you want to come?"

She bit her lip. It wouldn't take long, but she had waited so long to start work on the house. She didn't want to wait any longer.

"I think I'll stay here and start pulling up some of the weeds. Getting the yard looking nice will probably be the easiest thing I'm going to do here, but it's still going to take forever."

He gave her a kiss goodbye and she handed over her keys, pausing to get her pail of gardening supplies out of the bed of the truck before he left. He would be back in a few minutes, so even though she still felt a little unsettled here not knowing who killed Annabelle, she pulled on the same gardening gloves she had used to weed and plant the flower beds at home and got to work.

It was hard but satisfying work, and everything was going fine until she heard the scuff of a shoe on the sidewalk. She looked up, half expecting to see Wyatt or Willow coming over to say hello, but instead found herself face-to-face with Mason Mitchell, who was looking down at her from her driveway.

She rose to her feet quickly.

"Hi, Mr. Mitchell," she said. She reached for her phone in her back pocket, intending to call Jonah, then realized she had left it in the truck. She felt the first trickle of real unease slip down her spine. "What can I help you with?"

He looked perfectly normal, not like he was having some sort of memory episode. Maybe he was just taking a stroll around the neighborhood and wanted to see his old house.

Her hopes fell when he frowned at her, then looked past her at the door to the house and continued walking up the porch steps without saying a word.

"Hey, wait," she said, moving toward him. He ignored her, turning the doorknob and stepping inside.

Flora was frozen halfway up the porch steps. Should she follow him? Should she just wait for Grady to get back?

But she had already brought a lot of her tools inside. And obviously Jonah hadn't been lying; his father did have problems, which meant if he hurt himself on one of her power tools while invading her house, it would be her fault.

He was a confused old man. She was a relatively fit woman in her thirties. All she had to do was guide him out of the house and wait for Grady to get back with her cell phone.

Easy-peasy.

She pushed the front door open and stepped into the house.

CHAPTER TWELVE

"Mr. Mitchell? Mason?" Flora called out just inside the front door. He had already vanished, and the bare subfloors didn't give any hints as to where he had gone.

Her pile of power tools seemed untouched, though. That was good. Leaving the front door open, she hurried down the hall, checking the bathroom and the laundry room, then finally entering the kitchen, but each room was as empty as the last.

A dull thud from above her head was what finally gave his location away. He was upstairs. If she guessed correctly based on the location of the noise, he was in the room with the attic.

She took a deep breath. He was having a mental

health episode. He probably thought he still lived here. She should be sympathetic, not scared.

Before she started up the stairs, she heard a vehicle pull into the driveway. Good, Grady was back already. She waited until she heard a car door slam, then stuck her head down the hallway to call out, "Mr. Mitchell is here, I'm going upstairs to see if I can get him to come back down!"

Before he could answer, she hurried up the stairs. They had left the attic open and the ladder folded down, and she really didn't want him going up there.

"Mr. Mitchell?" she called out again at the top of the stairs. "Mason? It's Flora. Flora Abner. You sold this house to me, remember?"

She entered the biggest bedroom and there he was, standing in the closet with the light on, staring up at the attic's entrance.

"Why don't you come downstairs? We'll give Jonah a call –"

"Were you in the attic, son?"

The question startled her. Son? "I'm Flora, Mr. Mitchell, I'm not –"

Mason Mitchell turned around, looking at her but not quite seeing her. "You know you're not allowed in the attic. My house, my rules. I told you, there's bats up there. I can't afford an exterminator. You didn't go up there, did you?"

She heard footsteps on the stairs and breathed a sigh of relief. Grady was almost here. Grady would know how to handle this. Should she just play along? Pretend to be Jonah? Maybe that would be easier for him. Wasn't that what people were supposed to do when they had relatives with dementia?

"No?" she tried. "Um, Dad." This was so awkward. Jonah had said to explain what was going on if his father showed up, but she had tried that and he had completely ignored her.

She took a half step back at his intense gaze, feeling beyond uncomfortable with the situation.

"Remember not to go in the attic," he muttered, turning back to the closet. He paused and looked around. "We have to board it up again. No one can go up there."

"Why can't anyone go up there, Dad?"

Flora jumped, slapping her hands to cover her mouth as she shrieked and spun around to see Jonah standing in the doorway. The car she had heard pull up wasn't Grady after all – it was Mason Mitchell's son, the person who was either definitely the murderer or definitely not, depending on who she asked.

He winced and muttered an apology to her, but most of his attention was focused on his father. "Dad, why can't anyone go up there?"

"You know why," his father responded, still looking around for the boards. "The bats. I told you. You're still afraid of bats, aren't you?"

Flora glanced between them, biting her lip. A slow, horrible realization began to unfurl in her mind.

It sounded like Mason had been the one who boarded up the attic, and he didn't want anyone else going up there. No matter how obvious it seemed that Jonah was the killer, at least before her conversation with Kaycee, she had always been confused about why he would leave her body hidden up here when he learned his father was selling the house.

But Mason Mitchell had memory problems. He had told her has much at the title company, when they chatted briefly after the sale was complete.

A man with such severe memory issues might have forgotten that he had hidden a body in the attic until it was too late.

"No one's been in the attic for ten years, Dad," Jonah said. His voice sounded pained, and when she risked a glance at him, she saw him looking at his father like he had just gotten the worst news of his life. "I trusted you. I never even questioned why we suddenly had an infestation of bats right after my girl-friend disappeared. I mean, why would I ever think my own *father* had anything to do with that? When I heard where her body was found…" He trailed off and closed his eyes, taking a deep breath. "I told myself there had to be another explanation. The house was sitting empty for so long, maybe someone moved her body here after you moved out. But I was lying to myself. You're the one who killed her, aren't you?"

"What are you talking about?" Mason asked, turning to face his son.

"Annabelle, Dad," Jonah said, sounding exasper-ated even through his pain. "What happened to Annabelle?"

"People think you did it," Mason muttered. "I told them you didn't. My son's a good boy."

"The police know I had nothing to do with that." He glanced at Flora, as if he wanted to explain himself. "I was with another woman that night, someone I knew named Kaycee, and she gave a state-ment on my behalf."

"I know," she said, her voice almost a whisper. "I've been doing some digging. Everyone seems to blame someone… but no one blamed your Dad. Why would he kill her?"

Jonah flinched and turned his attention back to his

father. "I don't know," he said quietly. Raising his voice slightly, he said, "Dad, I know what you did to Annabelle. I want you to tell me why."

"You went into the attic, didn't you?" his father said. Anger flashed across his face, but quickly faded to an expression of pained resignation. "I never wanted you to find out, son. She was a nice girl. She would have been good for you. Not a troublemaker like that other one."

"So why did you kill her?" Jonah asked, his voice rising as he took a step forward.

"I never meant to. I thought she was the other one. Kaycee. You told me you were going out on a date. When I heard someone sneaking up that trellis to your room, I thought it was the girl you were seeing on the side. She was going to wreck your life. You should have gone off to college with Annabelle, not stayed here in this little town and wasted your life away. Annabelle was good for you. Kaycee just wanted to drag you down."

"Why are you saying all of this? You didn't kill Kaycee, you killed Annabelle," Jonah said. He took another step forward, his hands clenched into fists. "I want to know *why*."

"I don't think he meant to," Flora said quietly. She didn't want this to devolve into violence.

Jonah glanced back at her, frowning. Mason must have heard her, because he nodded slowly.

"I heard her climbing up the trellis. It was dark. I snuck into your room. When she opened the window, I shoved her off the side of the house. I didn't realize it was Annabelle until I went down to the yard and saw her face in the moonlight. The fall killed her." He paused for a moment, his head bowed. "I knew how much it would hurt you to see her like that. I couldn't let you get hurt and I didn't want you to be blamed for her death, so I emptied a box of linens and hid her in it. I was going to move her later, but there was never a good time with everyone watching us so closely. You were always so afraid of bats, and I figured I could keep you out of there if I told you we had an infestation and boarded it up. As the years went by, I almost managed to convince myself it never happened. I'm sorry, son. I'm so sorry."

Flora had never seen a man his age break down into tears and she wished she hadn't now. Jonah looked torn for a moment, then he turned his back on his father.

"I need to go downstairs before I do something I'll regret," he told Flora. "Can you call the police? I don't think I can do it. I know what he did now… but he's my dad. I just… can't."

"I don't have my phone on me." She felt dazed and kept looking between them. One terrible decision ten years ago had changed so many people's lives forever.

Wordlessly, he handed her his phone and went down the stairs. She followed him, not wanting to be alone upstairs with his father.

She was glad she had Officer Hendricks' number memorized, even though he was never going to let her live this down. She was willing to bet she was the most troublesome resident of Warbler, and she didn't even have a criminal record. Well, she'd gotten a couple of parking tickets back when she lived in Chicago, but those were paid off, and didn't count.

EPILOGUE

Flora let out a low whistle at sight of the price quote at the bottom of the contractor's email. He was subcontracting an HVAC specialist and a plumber to install the furnace and water heater at the yellow house. An inspection earlier this week had confirmed that the plumbing and ducts were all in good condition, so the work that needed to be done was limited, but it was still expensive.

It was doable, though. She had known fixing up the house was going to be expensive. With a little luck, once the furnace and the water heater were installed, she would be able to do everything else on her own or with Grady's help. Her only costs going forward should be supplies, not labor.

She accepted his offer and asked what date they

would be able to start, then leaned back in the comfy computer chair in her little office. She had only returned to the little yellow house a handful of times in the days following Mason Mitchell's arrest, mostly because the place was mobbed with local news crews and morbid sightseers, and she didn't want to be involved.

The mystery of Annabelle Morgan's disappearance had been solved after a decade of mystery, but for Flora, it all felt far too recent. She wondered if Kaycee would ever know Mason had been trying to kill *her*, not Annabelle. She hoped not. That would be difficult knowledge for anyone to live with.

The entire mess made her grateful for her easy, loving relationship with Grady. Star-crossed romances and tragedies were all great for stories and plays, but in real life, happily ever afters were so much better.

Soon, she would start giving the little yellow house the attention it deserved. Soon, she would transform a place of tragedy into a place of hope and cheer.

But not today. Today, she had a catio to start building, a boyfriend to meet for dinner, and a life of her own to get on with.